INVESTIGATIONS

AIRCRAFT AND FLIGHT

PETER MELLETT &
JOHN ROSTRON

CONSULTANT: CHRIS OXLADE

Published by Anness Publishing Ltd,
Blaby Road, Wigston, Leicestershire LE18 4SE

Email: info@anness.com

Web: www.annesspublishing.com

If you like the images in this book and would like
to investigate using them for publishing, promotions
or advertising, please visit our website
www.practicalpictures.com for more information.

Publisher: Joanna Lorenz
Managing Editor, Children's Books:
    Gilly Cameron Cooper
Project Editor: Jenni Rainford
Copy Editors: Charlotte Hurdman, Nigel Rodgers
    and Mary Pickles
Consultant: Chris Oxlade
Designers: Caroline Grimshaw and Michael Leaman
Photographer: John Freeman
Stylists: Marion Elliot and Melanie Williams
Picture Researcher: Liz Eddison
Illustrator: Dave Bowyer
We would like to thank the following children, and their parents, for appearing
    in this book: Emily Askew, Sara Barnes, Maria Bloodworth, David Callega,
    Aaron Dumetz, Laurence de Freitas, Alistair Fulton, Anton Goldbourne,
    Sasha Howarth, Jon Leming, Jessica Moxley, Ifunanya Obi, Emily Preddie,
    Elen Rhys, Nicola Twiner and Joe Westbrook
Editorial Reader: Penelope Goodare
Production Controller: Claire Rae

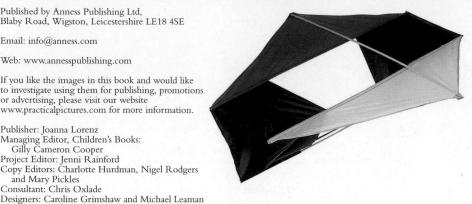

ETHICAL TRADING POLICY
Because of our ongoing ecological investment programme, you, as our customer, can
have the pleasure and reassurance of knowing that a tree is being cultivated on your
behalf to naturally replace the materials used to make the book you are holding.
For further information about this scheme, go to www.annesspublishing.com/trees

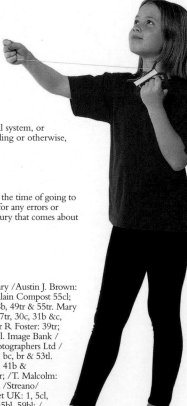

This is an expanded edition of *Learn About Flight*

PUBLISHER'S NOTE
Although the advice and information in this book are believed to be accurate and true at the time of going to
press, neither the authors nor the publisher can accept any legal responsibility or liability for any errors or
omissions that may have been made nor for any inaccuracies nor for any loss, harm or injury that comes about
from following instructions or advice in this book.

PICTURE CREDITS
(b=bottom, t=top, c=centre, l=left, r=right)
Cover front: Powerstock/Zefa; Stockmarket UK; Bruce Coleman.
back: Bruce Coleman/Alain Compost; Powerstock/Zefa; Papilio.
A – Z Botanical /Adrian Thomas: 36tr. Heather Angel: 54bl. The Aviation Picture Library /Austin J. Brown:
41t, 42tr & 58b. Bruce Coleman Ltd: 57bl; /Jane Burton: 54tl; /John Cancalosi: 56tl; /Alain Compost 55cl;
/Michael Kline: 19br; /Gordon Langsbury: 49br; /Hans Reinhard: 11t; /Kim Taylor: 48b, 49tr & 55tr. Mary
Evans Picture Library: 58t & c. The Flight Collection: 5t, 7br,11cl, 14tl, 24br, 25bl, br, 27tr, 30c, 31b &c,
35b, cl, 39c, tl, 40t, 41t, 42br, 43b, cr, 59t, 60t, 61t, bl; /Flight International: 21br; /Peter R Foster: 39tr;
/Trent Jones: 39b; /Erik Simonsen: 11cr & 4t; /Keith Wilson: 41br. Genesis: 13bl & 60cl. Image Bank /
Paul Bowen: 35tl; NASA: 35tr. NHPA: 48cr. Natural History Museum: 57c. Nature Photographers Ltd /
Roger Tidman: 7tl. Oxford Scientific Films: 32tl & 53c. Papillio Photographic: 4tr, 52bl, bc, br & 53tl.
Popperfoto: 43cl. Science Photo Library /Sam Ogden: 34br. Skyscan Photolibrary: 27tl, 41b &
endpaper. Spacecharts / Robin Kerrod: 4br, 46tl, 60b & 61c. Trip: 42bl; /T. Legate: 12br; /T. Malcolm:
24tl; /R. Marsh: 15bl; /Picturesque/Bill Terry: 11b; /P. Ridley: 17tl; /J. Ringland: 22br; /Streano/
Havens: 31tr; /TH-Foto Werbung: 16tl; /Derek Thomas: 21bl. Virgin: 22tr. Stockmarket UK: 1, 5cl,
7cl, 10tr, 15tl, tr, br, 17br, 21tl, 21tr, 52tl, 53tl, 55tl, b, 26tl, 30br, 34tr, 35cr, 38bl, 44tr, 45bl, 59bl; /
J. Sedlmeier: 59c.

Every effort has been made to trace the copyright holders of all images that appear
within this book. Anness Publishing Ltd apologises for any unintentional omissions and,
if notified, would be happy to add an acknowledgement in future editions.

INVESTIGATIONS

AIRCRAFT AND FLIGHT

CONTENTS

WHAT IS FLIGHT?

THINK OF flight and you may think of birds and insects, paper darts and aeroplanes, bullets and footballs. All of these can move swiftly through the air, but are they all really flying? To answer this question, imagine you are launching a paper dart into the air. It glides away from you and finally lands back on the ground. Now throw a ball in exactly the same way. It hits the ground much sooner than the paper dart. We say that the paper dart was flying, but the ball was not. This is because bullets, footballs, stones and arrows are all projectiles. They do not really fly because they have nothing to keep them up in the air. Birds, aircraft, rockets and balloons do fly – they stay off the ground longer than something that is simply thrown.

Animal power
Birds, insects and bats all have wings. These animals use their wings to hold themselves up in the air and move along. Muscles provide power for take-off.

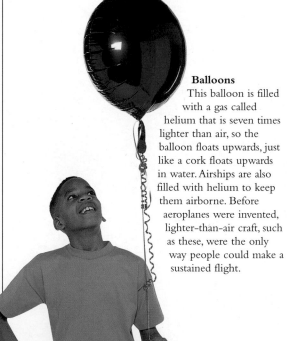

Balloons
This balloon is filled with a gas called helium that is seven times lighter than air, so the balloon floats upwards, just like a cork floats upwards in water. Airships are also filled with helium to keep them airborne. Before aeroplanes were invented, lighter-than-air craft, such as these, were the only way people could make a sustained flight.

Spaceflight
The space shuttle is launched into Space by powerful main engines and booster rockets. It uses smaller engines, as part of the orbital manoeuvring system, to increase speed, in order to reach an orbit about 300km above the Earth. The force of Earth's gravity acts like a tether, keeping the shuttle in orbit, while the shuttle's speed prevents it from falling back to the ground.

Aeroplanes

Like birds, aeroplanes have wings to hold them up in the air, but they also have engines. Engine power is needed to help them take off from the ground and push them through the air. Most long-distance aeroplanes fly at great heights because as air becomes less dense with height, drag is reduced so less thrust is needed to maintain speed. So the power and fuel needed to push them through the air is much less than at ground level. More fuel is needed during take-off as engines work at maximum thrust to gain height as quickly as possible.

Gliders

Since gliders have no engines, they have to be towed into the air by small aeroplanes or by machines on the ground. The towline is then released and the gliders' wings hold them up. In still air they will glide slowly back to the ground in a gentle spiral. The pilot controls the glider's flight by searching for rising air currents, called thermals, and by altering the shape of the glider's wings. Most gliding is done in a hilly landscape where the hills cause the air to rise. By using these air currents, a glider pilot can keep his plane aloft for many hours, so long as these rising currents persist.

Flying a kite

A kite is lifted into the air by a blowing wind. A long string called a tether holds the kite at an angle to the wind. The air rushes against the kite, pushing it upwards and keeping it in the air. If the wind drops or the tether breaks, the kite will fall back to the ground.

WINGS AND LIFT

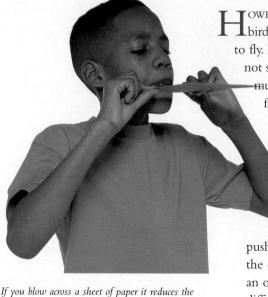

However much you flap your arms up and down like a bird, you cannot take off because you are not designed to fly. Humans are the wrong shape and their muscles are not strong enough. Birds have wings and powerful muscles that enable them to fly. Flapping provides a force called thrust, which moves a bird forwards through the air. A bird's wings are a special shape, called an aerofoil. In an aerofoil, the top side is more curved than the underneath. This helps to keep a bird up in the air, even when its wings are not flapping.

When an aerofoil wing moves through the air, it creates an upwards push. This push is a force called lift. It counteracts the weight of the object (due to the force of gravity), which pulls an object down towards the ground. There are many different shapes and sizes of birds, gliders and aeroplanes, but they all have aerofoil wings.

If you blow across a sheet of paper it reduces the pressure of the air above the paper. The stronger pressure beneath lifts the paper up.

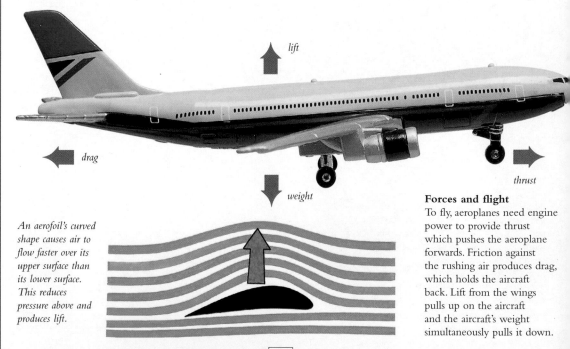

lift

drag

thrust

weight

An aerofoil's curved shape causes air to flow faster over its upper surface than its lower surface. This reduces pressure above and produces lift.

Forces and flight
To fly, aeroplanes need engine power to provide thrust which pushes the aeroplane forwards. Friction against the rushing air produces drag, which holds the aircraft back. Lift from the wings pulls up on the aircraft and the aircraft's weight simultaneously pulls it down.

Wings and soaring

A Lammergeyer can soar through the air without flapping its wings. As its wings slice through the air, the force of lift pushes up on them. The faster the bird's speed, the greater the lift. It is able to glide like this for many hours provided that it can maintain speed. Many seabirds can use the updraught near cliffs for this. Birds of the open ocean, such as the albatross, use variable air currents near the water surface, where the wind is slowed by contact with the water.

FACT BOX

• The jumbo jet Boeing 747-400, weighs nearly 400 tonnes on take-off. More than a third of this weight is fuel, which is stored in its wings. The jet has a wingspan of 64.4m.

• Most helicopters have between three and six rotor blades. The blades are more than 10m long, but only about 0.5m wide.

• A jumbo jet reaches a speed of almost 300km/h when it is taking off.

• Nearly a quarter of a pigeon's weight is taken up by the flight muscles needed to flap its wings.

• A boomerang is a bent aerofoil wing. The oldest boomerang in the world is 20,000 years old and was found in a cave in Poland.

Rotation

Helicopters have long thin aerofoil wings called rotor blades. Powerful engines whirl the blades to produce lift. Helicopters can hover, or fly forwards, backwards and sideways, as well as straight up and down. The pilot can position the angle of the blades to control lift and make the helicopter go in any direction. Because the rotor blades are continually spinning in one direction, the helicopter tends to rotate the other way. Most helicopters have a small propeller at the end of their body to help prevent this. Large helicopters may have a set of rotor blades at each end of the aircraft.

Taking off

Most aeroplanes need long runways to take off. They speed along, faster and faster, until the lift pushing up is greater than the weight pulling down, allowing them to leave the ground.

CURVE AND LIFT

FLY A FRISBEE

You will need: a large plate, thick card, pencil, scissors, ruler, sticky tape.

B IRDS, GLIDERS and aeroplanes all have wings. Their wings can be all sorts of different shapes and sizes, but they all have the same aerofoil design. This means that the top side of the wing is more curved than the underneath. The aerofoil shape provides lift when air moves over it. Air flows faster over the curved upper surface than over the flatter, lower surface. This reduces the air pressure above the wing and allows the higher air pressure underneath to lift it up.

You can make and test a model aerofoil by following the instructions in these projects. They will show you how moving air lifts wings upwards. In the first, disc-shaped frisbee project, the curve at the top and bottom is the same, but because the top curves outwards, air can move faster over the top of it. The frisbee spins as it flies. The spinning motion and speed help to steady it.

1 Place the plate face down on the card and draw around it with a pencil. Cut out the circle of card. Draw slots 2cm deep around the edge and cut along these as shown.

2 The cut slots around the edge will make tabs. Bend the tabs down slightly. Overlap them a little and stick them together with small pieces of sticky tape.

3 Fly your frisbee outside, away from people. Hold it at the front and spin it away from you and up. It should glide through the air smoothly as the air pressure above it is reduced. Play toss-and-catch games with your friends and even have your own championship match. Commercial frisbees were introduced into the United States in the 1950s.

AEROFOIL ANTICS

You will need: paper, pencil, ruler, scissors, sticky tape, glue, plastic drinking straw, thick cotton yarn.

1 Measure a rectangle of paper about 15cm wide and 20cm long. Carefully cut out the shape.

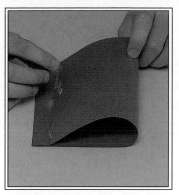

2 Fold the paper over, approximately in half. Use sticky tape to stick the top edge 1cm away from the bottom edge.

3 Cut out and stick on a small fin near the rear edge of your wing. This will keep the wing facing into the airflow when you test it.

4 With a sharp pencil, poke a hole through the top and bottom of your wing, near the front edge. Push a straw through the holes and glue it in place in the middle.

6 Hold the cotton tight and blow air from a fan or hair dryer over the wing. Watch it take off! This happens because you are decreasing the air pressure above the wing.

5 Cut a 1m long piece of thick cotton yarn and thread it through the straw. Make sure the cotton can slide easily through the straw and does not catch.

AIR RESISTANCE

WHEN YOU are swimming, you push your way through the water. All the time, the water is resisting you and slowing you down. In the same way, things that fly have to push their way through the air. Air also clings to their surfaces as they rush through it. The result is a backwards pull called drag, or air resistance. Drag is the force that works against the direction of flight of anything that is flying through the air. The amount of drag depends on shape. Fat, lumpy shapes with sharp edges create a lot of drag. They disturb the air and make it swirl about as they move along. Sleek, streamlined shapes have low drag and hardly disturb the air as they cut smoothly through it so they fly fastest of all.

Whatever the shape, drag increases with speed. Doubling the speed creates four times the amount of drag. The result is that drag limits how fast aircraft, birds and insects can fly, increasing the amount of thrust needed.

Trapped air
Parachutes fall slowly because air is trapped beneath them. They are deliberately designed to have very high drag.

When an aircraft is in flight, the angle the wings make to the airflow is called the angle of attack. If the angle of attack is increased, the amount of lift also increases – but so does the drag.

angle of attack

If the angle of attack becomes too great, lift drops suddenly. The smooth flow of air over the wing is broken, creating turbulence, increasing drag and reducing lift.

turbulence

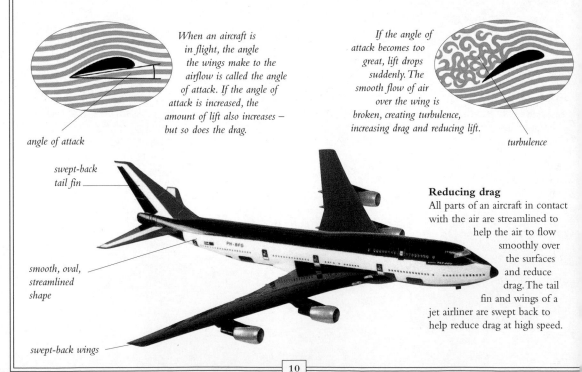

swept-back
tail fin

smooth, oval,
streamlined
shape

swept-back wings

Reducing drag
All parts of an aircraft in contact with the air are streamlined to help the air to flow smoothly over the surfaces and reduce drag. The tail fin and wings of a jet airliner are swept back to help reduce drag at high speed.

Coming in to land

Birds must slow down before they land. This owl has tipped up its wings so that the undersides face forwards. It has also lowered and spread out its tail feathers to act as a brake. Drag increases suddenly, lift decreases and the bird drops to its landing place.

High speed

Concorde can fly at a speed of over 2,000km/h. Its wings are swept back to reduce drag to a minimum. If its wings stuck straight out they would be ripped off at this speed.

Parachute brakes

The Lockheed SR-71 lands at over 350km/h. A parachute helps it slow down, as ordinary brakes on its wheels would take too long.

Down to earth

Coming in to land, an airliner uses flaps on its wings to increase lift at low speeds. During flight, these flaps are retracted (pulled in) to reduce drag.

SHAPED BY DESIGN

THINK OF a sleek canoe moving through water. Its streamlined shape makes hardly any ripples as it passes by. Streamlined shapes also move easily through air. We say that they have low drag, or air resistance. Angular shapes have more drag than rounded ones. For effective streamlining, think about the shape of fast-moving fishes which have to be very streamlined. A fish such as a tuna has a blunt front end, is broadest about a third of the way along, then tapers towards the tail. This is more streamlined than a shape with a pointed front end and thicker at the other end because it creates least drag as it moves through water. It splits the water cleanly, allowing it to flow along each side of the tuna to rejoin without creating turbulence. In these experiments, you can design and test your own streamlined shapes, or make a model parachute with high drag to make it fall slowly.

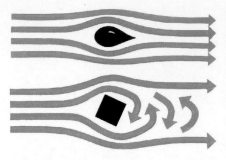

How it works
Air flows in gentle curves around the streamlined shape (top). Angles or sharp curves break up the flow and increase drag.

star   *square*   *teardrop*

Shape race
Make different shapes (*as shown on the right*) from balls of modelling clay all the same size. Race your shapes in water – the most streamlined shape should reach the bottom first.

Splash down
How much of a splash would you make diving into a pool? This diver's carefully streamlined shape will help her cut cleanly through the water to dive deeply.

MINI PARACHUTE JUMP

You will need: *felt-tipped pen, a large plate, thin fabric, scissors, needle, cotton thread, sticky tape, plastic cotton reel.*

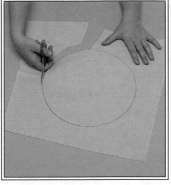

1 Use the felt-tipped pen to draw around the plate on the fabric. Using the scissors, carefully cut out the circle to make what will be the parachute's canopy.

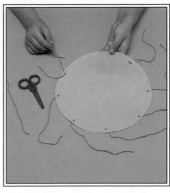

2 Make about eight equally spaced marks around the edge of the circle. Use a needle to sew on one 30cm long piece of cotton thread to each point you have marked.

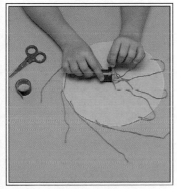

3 Use sticky tape to secure the free end of each thread to a cotton reel. Make sure you use a plastic cotton reel, as a wooden one will be too heavy for your parachute.

4 Let your parachute go from as high up as possible. As it falls, the canopy will open and fill with air. The larger the canopy, the slower the parachute will fall.

Holey parachute

Parachutes today have a hole in the centre. This one brought two *Apollo 17* astronauts safely to land in the Pacific Ocean. The hole ensures that the air escapes evenly instead of at the sides, which would cause swinging.

GLIDING AND SOARING

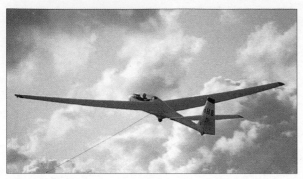

Long, thin wings
A glider is towed into the air attached to a cable. Its long, thin wings give maximum lift and minimum drag for their size. If a glider flies level in still air, drag forces slow it down and the wings lose their lift. So, to keep up speed, a glider flies on a gradual downward slope.

WATCH A small bird as it flies. It flaps its wings very fast for almost the whole time. Large birds, however, often glide with their wings stretched out flat and unmoving. They can do this because their large wings create enough lift to keep them up in the air without flapping. Soaring birds, such as albatrosses and condors, glide for hours hardly moving their wings at all. They gain height by using thermals (rising columns of hot air) over the land and sea. Gliders are aircraft that do not have engines. Instead they have long, thin wings, similar to those of soaring birds. They are pulled along by small aircraft or by winches on the ground, until the lift generated by their wings keeps them airborne. Glider pilots also seek out thermals to lift their aircraft up.

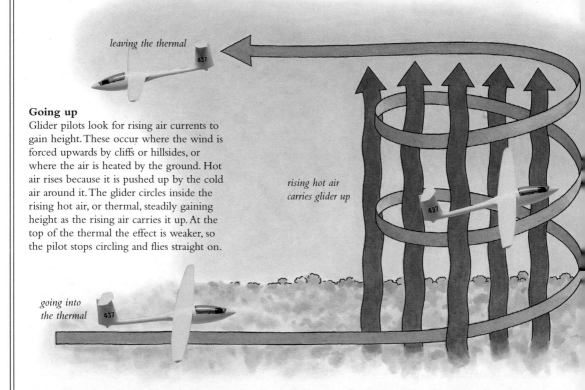

leaving the thermal

Going up
Glider pilots look for rising air currents to gain height. These occur where the wind is forced upwards by cliffs or hillsides, or where the air is heated by the ground. Hot air rises because it is pushed up by the cold air around it. The glider circles inside the rising hot air, or thermal, steadily gaining height as the rising air carries it up. At the top of the thermal the effect is weaker, so the pilot stops circling and flies straight on.

rising hot air carries glider up

going into the thermal

Flying high

The wing shape of a paraglider is made by air blowing into pockets on its leading edge. The pilot steers from side to side and can ride up thermals.

Wingspan

Albatrosses have long narrow wings. This wing shape helps them to glide for enormous distances on air currents blowing over the open ocean. Albatrosses have the longest wingspan of any bird, measuring over 3m from tip to tip.

Hang-glider

A hang-glider is made from strong, thin material stretched over a framework of aluminium poles and is very light. The material on the hang-glider's wing is stretched into an aerofoil shape to produce lift. To steer the hang-glider, the pilot moves a control bar forwards to climb and backwards to dive. Hang-gliders are often launched by the pilot simply jumping off the edge of a cliff where an updraught of air will provide the necessary lift. Because of the pilot's all-round vision, hang-gliders are used for aerial surveys and observation.

Cockpit dials

This picture shows the inside of a glider's cockpit. The left-hand dial gives forward air speed. The middle dial shows the rate of climb or descent (how fast the glider is going up or down). The last dial on the right shows the glider's altitude (height above the ground).

KITES AND SAILS

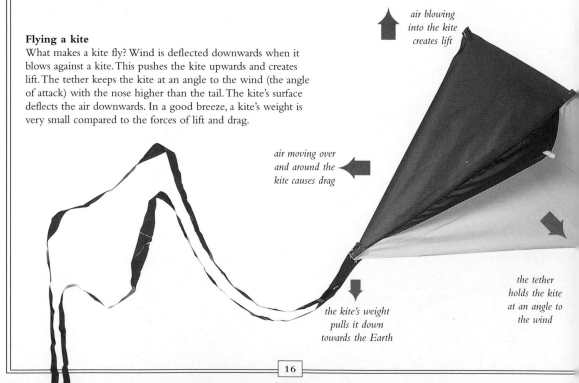

W IND IS moving air that pushes against anything standing in its path. You can fly a kite because it is held up in the air by the force of the wind pushing against it. A string, called a tether, joins the kite to the person flying it and holds it at the correct angle to the wind. You can feel tension in the tether pulling on your hand. The tension is the result of the wind blowing against the kite and lifting it up. If the tether broke, the kite would no longer be held at the correct angle and it would fall to the ground or blow away. When there is no wind, a kite can still be made to fly by pulling it through the air. A simple kite like the one below will also need a tail. This tail provides extra drag and ensures that the kite always faces into the wind at the correct angle so it can create lift. Traditionally, kite tails have many tassels along their length. These also add to the drag and mean that the tail does not need to be so long.

Open mouthed
Windsock kites may be flown from poles during festivals. They have open ends to catch the wind. Like all kites, they only fly when the wind blows against them.

Flying a kite
What makes a kite fly? Wind is deflected downwards when it blows against a kite. This pushes the kite upwards and creates lift. The tether keeps the kite at an angle to the wind (the angle of attack) with the nose higher than the tail. The kite's surface deflects the air downwards. In a good breeze, a kite's weight is very small compared to the forces of lift and drag.

air blowing
into the kite
creates lift

air moving over
and around the
kite causes drag

the tether
holds the kite
at an angle to
the wind

the kite's weight
pulls it down
towards the Earth

Flat kite

The oldest and simplest kite is the plane surface, or flat, kite. It has a simple diamond shape and a flat frame. Kites like these have been flown for thousands of years. Flat kites look very impressive strung together to make a writhing pattern in the sky.

Box kite

A square box kite is more complicated to make than a flat kite. Its shape makes it more stable and gives it better lift. It does not need a tail to keep it upright. Box kites can be a combination of triangles and rectangles. Large box kites have been used to lift people off the ground in the past.

Parasail

A parasail is a kite that lifts a person into the air. It does not rely completely on the wind, but instead it is towed behind a boat or a car. A parasail looks like a parachute that has been divided into different parts, called cells. As the parasail is pulled along, air flows into each separate cell, inflating it to make a shape that creates lift. Parasails usually fly about 50m above the ground.

LET'S GO FLY A KITE

FOR MORE than 3,000 years, people have been making and flying kites. The first ones were made from cloth or paper attached to a light wooden or bamboo frame. As time went by, the essential but simple secret of building a good kite was discovered. It must be as light as possible for its size, so that it catches as much wind as possible. Some kites can fly in remarkably gentle breezes. Their surfaces are wide so that the breeze has a large area to push against. Their low weight means that only a small amount of lift is enough to make them take off into the sky.

The Chinese have for long made some of the most elaborate and colourful kites of all. In Tibet and some other Himalayan regions, kite-flying is often a part of religious festivities. Competitions to see whose kite flies or looks best are now organized in many countries around the world. The kite design shown in this project has been used for many hundreds of years. Try flying it first of all in a steady wind. You might have to experiment with the position of the bridle and the length of the tail.

MAKE A KITE

You will need: pen, ruler, two plant canes (one about two-thirds as long as the other), string, scissors, sticky tape, sheet of thin fabric or plastic, fabric glue, coloured paper.

1 To make the frame, mark the centre of the short cane and mark one-third of the way up the long cane. Tie the canes together crossways at the marks with string.

2 Tape string around the ends of the canes and secure it at the top. This will stop the canes from moving and it will also support the edges of your kite.

3 Lay the frame on top of the sheet of material or plastic. Cut around it, 3cm away from the material's edge. This will give you enough to fold over the string outline.

4 Fold each edge of the material over the frame and stick the edges down firmly with fabric glue (or sticky tape if you are making the kite from plastic). Leave the glue to dry.

5 Tie a piece of string to the long cane, as shown – this is called the bridle. Tie the end of the ball of string to the middle of the bridle to make the tether.

6 To make the tail, fold sheets of coloured paper in zigzags. Tie them at about 25cm intervals along a piece of string that is about twice as long as the kite. Glue or tie the tail to the bottom tip of the kite.

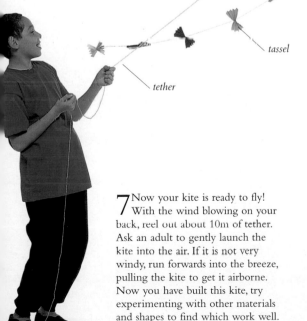

bridle

tail

tassel

tether

7 Now your kite is ready to fly! With the wind blowing on your back, reel out about 10m of tether. Ask an adult to gently launch the kite into the air. If it is not very windy, run forwards into the breeze, pulling the kite to get it airborne. Now you have built this kite, try experimenting with other materials and shapes to find which work well.

Flying faces
This kite has been made to look like a face with a long trailing moustache. Highly decorative designs can make the simplest kite look very effective.

LIGHTER THAN AIR

Hot stuff
A candle heats the air around it. Even after you snuff out the flame the smoke is carried upwards by the hot air.

OIL FLOATS on water because it is the lighter and less dense of the two liquids. A bottle full of oil weighs less than the same bottle full of water. Water pushes upwards on the oil with a force called upthrust. A similar process happens when smoke rises from a fire. Hot air is less dense than the cold air around it and is forced up by the cold air. It floats upwards, taking the smoke with it.

A hot-air balloon is simply a huge bag full of hot air. It experiences upthrust from the cold air around it. The balloon takes off because the upthrust is greater than its own weight pulling it down. Airships are also lighter than the air around them. Modern airships are filled with a gas called helium, which is seven times lighter than air. The hot air in a balloon gradually escapes or cools down, however, so the pilot needs to regularly produce more by burning gas underneath it. The hot gases from a single gas cylinder can carry several people for half an hour.

Oil slick
Watch how oil floats on water because it is less dense than air. The water surrounding the oil pushes upwards on it. This push is called upthrust. Try this with a glass of water and a teaspoon of cooking oil.

FACT BOX
• The first ever balloon passengers were not humans but a sheep, a duck and a cockerel, in 1782, at the Court of Versailles, in Paris. They were sent up to make sure it was safe to travel by this new form of transport.

• The first untethered balloon flight took place over Paris on 21 November 1783. It lasted only 25 minutes but reached 500m.

• Marie Elisabeth Thible became the first woman aeronaut. On 4 June 1784, she flew in a balloon over Lyon, France.

• One of the largest airships was the German *Hindenburg*, at 244m long. In 1937, it burst into flames on landing, killing 35 people.

The first aviators

In 1783, French brothers Joseph and Jacques Montgolfier built an enormous paper balloon and lit a fire on the ground beneath it. The air inside the balloon gradually cooled after take-off. The balloon sailed into the sky, safely carrying two people into the air for the very first journey by hot-air balloon. By 1784, refined versions of their balloon could carry six people.

Hanging baskets

Modern hot-air balloons are as tall as an eight-storey block of flats. They are made of nylon and can carry about five people in a basket hanging underneath. All hot-air balloons can only go where the wind blows them. This means pilots must have a landing site arranged downwind before setting off!

Danger

Airships in the 1930s were huge, being designed to carry passengers across the Atlantic in luxury. They were filled with hydrogen gas that easily burst into flames, making the airships very dangerous. Today airships use helium.

Modern airship

Unlike a hot-air balloon, this airship uses helium to float. It also has engines and propellers to drive it. The pilot steers by moving fins on the tail.

HOT AIR RISING

HOT AIR BALLOONS rise into the sky because the air inside them is lighter than the air outside. The main part of the balloon is called the envelope. Hot air rises into the envelope from gas burners stored just beneath the envelope but above the basket. The number of gas cylinders stored in the basket depends on the journey time. The envelope fills with about 2.5 tonnes of hot air – about the weight of two cars. This hot air pushes cold, more dense air around the balloon, out of the way, producing enough upthrust to lift the balloon, its passengers and bottles of gas off the ground.

You can make and fly a model hot-air balloon to see it rise in exactly the same way. However, do not attempt to fill your balloon using flames of any sort. Modern hot-air balloons are made of flame-resistant fabric so that they do not melt or catch fire, especially during the process of filling the balloon with hot air. The best material for a home-made balloon is coloured tissue paper. You can easily produce hot air without using flames by using a hair dryer.

A super challenge
Virgin *Challenger* is capable of flying journeys of thousands of kilometres. Once the balloon is high into the atmosphere, the strong winds of a jet stream (fast moving, high altitude winds) carry it along.

Stabilize a balloon
Try adding modelling clay to the string of a helium balloon until the balloon hangs steady. The force downwards (weight) now equals the force upwards (upthrust).

Gas burners
Roaring gas burners heat the air. The hot air rises to fill the balloon's envelope, which takes more than half an hour. When the envelope is full, the balloon is launched by untying ropes that hold it to the ground.

BALLOONING AROUND

You will need: pencil, card, ruler, scissors, sheets of tissue paper, glue stick, hair dryer.

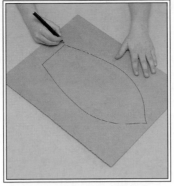

1 Draw a petal-shaped template on card and cut it out. The shape should be 30cm long and 12cm across with a flat bottom edge.

2 Draw around your template on seven pieces of tissue paper. Be careful not to rip the paper with the tip of your pencil.

3 Use the pair of scissors to carefully cut out the shapes you have drawn. You should now have seven petals that are all the same size and shape.

4 Glue along one edge of a petal. Lay another petal on top and press down. Open out and stick on another petal in the same way. Keep going until the balloon is complete.

5 To fly your balloon, hold its neck open and fill the inside with hot air from a hair dryer. After ten seconds, switch off the hair dryer and let go of your balloon to launch it into the air.

WHAT'S IN A WING?

Triplane
This aircraft is called a triplane because it has three sets of wings. Early planes needed more sets of wings to provide enough lift as their speed was slow. Some very early planes were built with five or more sets of wings, but they were never successful.

THE SMALLEST microlight aircraft carries one person and weighs less than 100kg. The largest passenger jet carries over 500 people and weighs nearly 400 tonnes. Whatever the size or shape, all aeroplanes have wings in common. Wings provide the lift they need to hold them in the air. The shape of the wings depends on how fast and high an aircraft needs to fly.

Narrow wings can reduce the amount of drag, and so are better for high-speed flight. Drag can also be reduced by having swept-back wings. However, wings like this are not as efficient when taking off and landing. To carry heavy loads, the aeroplane needs high lift which is provided by a large wing area. Passenger and cargo planes have broad (medium-length) wings, slightly swept back. All wings have moving parts to help the aeroplane land, take off, slow down and change direction.

tail fin

wing

propeller

tailplane

fuselage

undercarriage

The parts of an aircraft
Each of the main parts of a small aircraft labelled here plays a part in helping the aircraft to take off, fly level, change direction and land. The body of the aircraft is called the fuselage and the landing wheels are called the undercarriage. On many aircraft, the undercarriage folds up inside the body of the aircraft during flight to reduce drag. Hinged control surfaces on the tail and the wings are used to steer the aircraft from left to right as well as up and down.

Piper Cadet
Most aeroplanes today are monoplanes. A monoplane has one set of wings. The wings of small planes such as this Piper Cadet stick straight out from the aircraft's body, because at speeds of only a few hundred km/h they do not need to be swept back, and this way they provide the greatest lift. These planes fly only short distances at a height of a no greater than a kilometre.

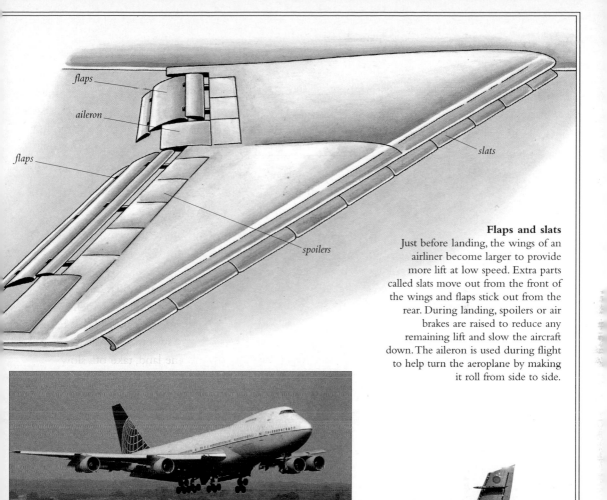

flaps

aileron

flaps

slats

spoilers

Flaps and slats
Just before landing, the wings of an airliner become larger to provide more lift at low speed. Extra parts called slats move out from the front of the wings and flaps stick out from the rear. During landing, spoilers or air brakes are raised to reduce any remaining lift and slow the aircraft down. The aileron is used during flight to help turn the aeroplane by making it roll from side to side.

Boeing 747
Wide-bodied jets, such as this Boeing 747, fly high and fast. Large wings provide enough lift to carry nearly 400 tonnes, more than a third of which is the aircraft's fuel. The wings are tapered and swept back to keep drag low when flying at 1,000km/h. Swept-back wings reduce lift, so a high take-off speed is needed, but by reducing drag they also reduce fuel consumption. Even so, in one hour, a Boeing 747's engines burn 8,000 litres aviation fuel, which is enough to run a family car for six years.

Swing-wings
Some military aircraft can move their wings. For high-speed flight, wings are swept backwards in a low-drag triangle shape. To provide lift at lower speeds, the wings are swung forwards.

TAKING FLIGHT

To make a car turn left or right, all you have to do is turn the steering wheel. To steer a light aircraft, you must move two sets of controls, one with your hands and one with your feet. Moving these controls alters the control surfaces on the plane's wings and tail. Control surfaces are small hinged flaps that affect how air flows around the plane. There are three main types of control surface. Ailerons are attached to the rear edge of each wing. Elevators are mounted at the rear of the tailplane and the rudder is at the rear of the tail fin.

Double power
Biplanes have two sets of wings. They are strong, agile and easy to fly and are often used as trainer planes or in acrobatic displays. Biplanes with open cockpits and wings braced with wires and struts were the most common aeroplane design until the 1930s. Then, monoplanes (with single wings) replaced them in almost all functions.

The pilot can also control flight by engine power – more power increases speed and so increases lift. So, an accelerating aircraft flying level will steadily gain height.

In a large or fast aircraft, controls are operated either electrically or hydraulically. The pilot can send electrical signals to small motors which operate the controls, or they can be hydraulically controlled by pumping fluid along pipes inside cylinders to operate them.

Control surfaces
To turn the aircraft (yaw), the pilot turns the rudder to one side. To make the aircraft descend or climb (pitch), the pilot adjusts the elevators on the tailplane. To roll (tilt or bank) the aircraft to the right or left, the ailerons are raised on one wing and lowered on the other.

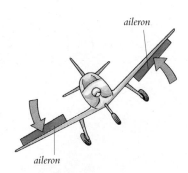

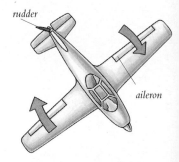

Roll
The ailerons operate in opposite directions to each other to tilt the aircraft as it turns. When one aileron is raised, the other is lowered. The wing with the lowered aileron then rises while the wing with the raised aileron automatically drops.

Pitch
The elevators on the plane's tail are raised or lowered to alter the pitch of the plane. Lowering the elevators causes the aircraft's nose to drop, putting the plane into a dive. Raising them causes the aircraft to climb.

Yaw
The rudder works with the ailerons to adjust the yaw. When the yaw is swivelled to one side the aircraft moves to the left or the right. Whichever way it points, the aircraft's nose (at the front) is turned in the same direction as the yaw.

Bank on it

When an aircraft turns, it moves rather like a cyclist going round a corner. It banks as it turns, which means that it leans to one side with one wing higher than the other. This means that some of the lift from the wings is used to turn the aircraft.

In the cockpit

Inside the cockpit of a modern airliner, the pilot moves throttle levers to control engine power. The control column and pedals move the control surfaces. Dials and gauges give information such as fuel consumption, flight direction, altitude and how level the plane is flying.

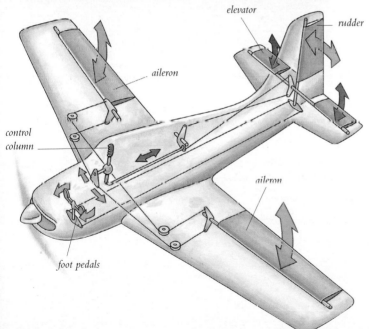

elevator

rudder

aileron

control column

aileron

foot pedals

In command

To control the aircraft, the pilot moves the control column from side to side to operate the ailerons. Moving the control column backwards or forwards operates the elevators. The foot pedals move the rudder from side to side.

FACT BOX
• Many flight terms are borrowed from terms used on board ships, including yaw, pitch and roll, port (left) and starboard (right).

• It takes an airliner one minute and nearly 2km of airspace to reverse its course.

• A cruising airliner loses 3 tonnes in weight every hour as fuel is used up.

• Many aircraft use computer–controlled autopilot systems. These fly the aircraft automatically from one place to another.

• To control a helicopter, the angle of the rotor blades is adjusted. This allows the aircraft to hover, go straight upwards, forwards, backwards or even sideways.

MODEL PLANES

Paper aeroplanes
You can make model planes with nothing but paper. They can vary from a simple paper dart to a glider with separate wings and a tailplane. To make a successful paper plane, you need to use stiff paper (not card), so that it will hold its shape. You can also cut ailerons in the rear edges of the wings to adjust the flight as described in the project below.

WE HAVE seen how the control surfaces on the wings and the tail of an aircraft work – they change the way air flows over the aircraft, allowing the pilot to steer the aircraft in different directions. Working together, the ailerons and rudder make the plane turn to the left or right. Moving elevators on the tail make the nose of the plane go up or down. Although a model is much smaller than a real full-size aircraft, it flies in exactly the same way.

The scientific rules of flying are the same for any aircraft, from an airliner weighing 350 tonnes to this model made from pieces of paper, sticky tape and a drinking straw. Making this model plane allows you to see how control surfaces such as the aileron, rudder and elevators work. The flight of any plane, including your model, is sensitive to the angle of the controls. They need be only a slight angle from their flat position to make the plane turn. Too big an angle will make the model unstable.

GLIDE ALONG

You will need: pencil, set square, ruler, paper, scissors, glue, sticky tape, drinking straw, paper clip.

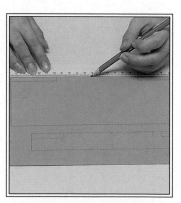

1 Draw two paper rectangles, 22 x 10cm and 20 x 4cm. Mark ailerons 6 x 1cm on two corners of the larger one. Mark two elevators 4 x 1cm on the other. Cut them out.

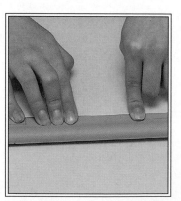

2 To make the wings, wrap the larger rectangle over a pencil and glue along the edges. Remove the pencil and make cuts along the 1cm lines to allow the ailerons to move.

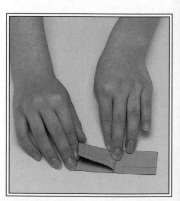

3 To make the tail, fold the smaller rectangle in half twice to form a W. Glue its centre to make the fin. Cut along the two 1cm lines. Make a 1cm cut on the fin to make a rudder.

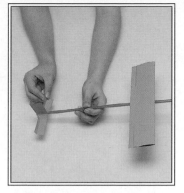

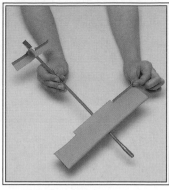

4 Use sticky tape to stick the wings and tail to the straw (the plane's fuselage or body). Position the wings about one quarter of the way along the fuselage.

5 Try adjusting the control surfaces. Bend the elevators on the tail up slightly. This will make the plane climb as it flies. Bend the elevators down to make it dive.

6 Bend the left-hand aileron up and the right-hand aileron down the same amount. Bend the rudder to the left. This will make the plane turn to the left as it flies.

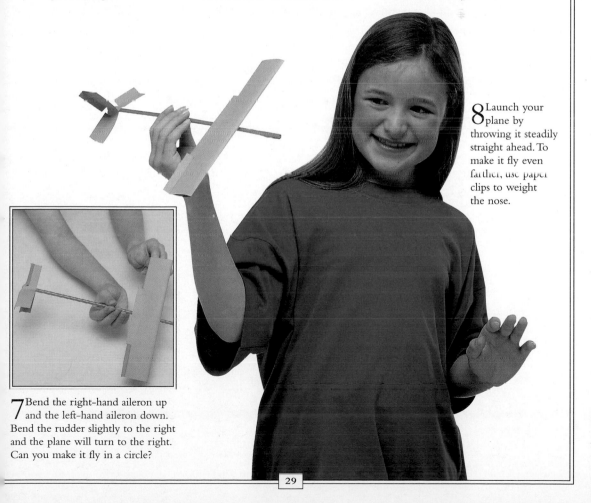

8 Launch your plane by throwing it steadily straight ahead. To make it fly even farther, use paper clips to weight the nose.

7 Bend the right-hand aileron up and the left-hand aileron down. Bend the rudder slightly to the right and the plane will turn to the right. Can you make it fly in a circle?

PROPELLERS

ALL AIRCRAFT need thrust to push them through the air. A propeller whirling at high speed creates thrust. Propellers have two or more blades, each of which is shaped like a long, thin aerofoil wing. The blades generate lift in a forward direction as they move through the air. Modern propellers have variable-pitch blades, which means the pilot can alter the angle at which they bite into the air. Changing the pitch of a propeller is like changing gears on a bicycle. For take-off, the front of the blades point forwards and the engine spins very fast to generate maximum thrust. Less thrust is needed when cruising, so the blades are set at a sharper angle and the engine spins more slowly. This arrangement gives the most economical use of fuel.

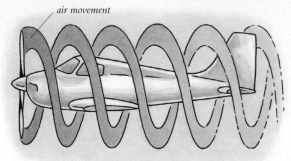

air movement

Air strike
Propellers screw their way through the air, in the same way a screw goes into wood. For this reason, aircraft driven by propellers are often known as airscrews. As the propeller turns, the blades strike the air and push it backwards. This produces thrust and moves the aircraft forwards.

Early racers
Sir Geoffrey De Havilland designed many early aircraft. The De Havilland DH-88 Comet took part in a race from England to Australia in 1934. It is shown here after it was restored for the fiftieth anniversary of the race. Each propeller is driven by a separate engine. Each one is like a huge car engine and is fuelled by petrol.

DH-88 Comet

Wooden propellers
The first aeroplanes had propellers made from layers of wood that were glued together. The pilot would spin the propeller by hand to start the engine. This was a very dangerous job because there was a chance that the pilot might be hit by the fast-spinning propeller.

Microlight

If you attach an engine-driven propeller to a hang-glider, the result is a microlight. The engine in this microlight aircraft develops about the same power as a small family car. The twin-bladed propeller is less than 1m across. It pushes the plane along at around 65km/h. Microlight aircraft are often used for survey work in remote parts of the world. The aircraft can be carried by road and then launched to survey areas far from the road.

Training planes

The Piper Seneca has four seats, so it can carry a pilot and three passengers. Aircraft like these are typically used for learning to fly. Like a car, they can be equipped with dual controls for trainer and learner. The propellers each have two blades. They are twisted at an angle like the blades of a fan. As the propellers spin, the blades force air backwards.

Piper Seneca

Lockheed Hercules

Heavy-duty carriers

This aircraft carries military supplies. Each propeller has four variable-pitch blades. The propellers are driven by a turboprop engine, a type of jet engine in which the hot gases drive a turbine, which in turn drives the propeller. There is also some thrust provided by the fast-moving exhaust gases.

PROPEL YOURSELF

To and fro
A boomerang is a special form
of spinner. Each of the two arms
is an aerofoil shape. When it is
thrown correctly, a boomerang will
fly in a circle, eventually returning to
the thrower.

PROPELLERS WORK in two different ways. When a propeller
spins, it makes air move past it. At the same time, the moving
air makes the propeller spin. Propeller-driven aircraft use this effect
to produce thrust. These projects look at propellers working in
these two ways. In the first you can make a simple paper propeller
called a spinner. As the spinner falls, moving air rushes past the
blades, making it revolve. This acts just like the fruits and seeds of
maple and sycamore trees which have two propeller blades. As
they drop from the tree, they spin and catch the wind, and are
carried far away.

In the second project, you can make a spinning propeller fly
upwards through the air. The propeller-like blades are set at an angle,
like the blades of a fan. They whirl around and make air move.
The moving air produces thrust and lifts the propeller upwards.
Children first flew propellers like these, 600 years ago in China.

IN A SPIN

You will need:
thin paper, ruler, pencil,
scissors, paper clip.

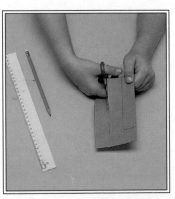

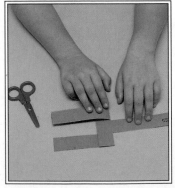

1 Take a piece of paper,
15cm x 9cm, and draw a T shape
on it, as shown in the picture above.
With a pair of scissors, cut along
the two long lines of the T.

2 Fold one side strip forwards and
one backwards, as shown above,
making two blades and a stalk.
Attach a paper clip to the bottom.
Open the blades flat.

3 Now drop the spinner - what
happens? Before dropping it
again, try giving each blade a
twist to make your spinner spin
round faster.

LET'S TWIST

You will need: *thick card, ruler, pair of compasses, protractor, pen, scissors, 1cm slice of cork, bradawl, 8cm length of 3mm diameter dowel, model glue, cotton reel, string.*

1 With the compasses, draw a circle about 10cm across on the card. Draw a smaller circle 2cm across in the centre. With the protractor, draw lines across the circle, dividing it into 16 equal sections.

2 Carefully cut out the circle and along the lines to the smaller circle. Twist the blades sideways a little. Try to give each blade the same amount of twist, about 20 to 30 degrees.

3 Make a hole in the centre of the cork slice with a bradawl. Put glue on the end of the dowel and push it into the hole. Stick the cork in the middle of the propeller.

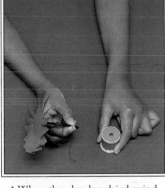

4 When the glue has dried, wind a long piece of string around the dowel. Drop the dowel into the cotton reel launcher. You are now ready for a test flight.

5 Pull steadily on the string to whirl the propeller around. As the end of the string comes away, the blades produce enough thrust to lift the spinning propeller out of the launcher and into the air.

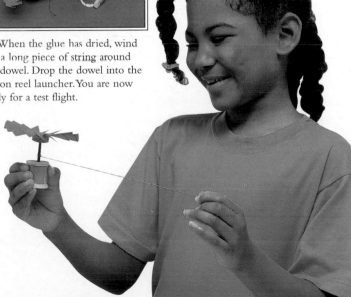

JET ENGINES

MOST LARGE modern aircraft are driven by jet engines. They fly faster than aeroplanes with propellers because they can fly high where the air is thin and drag is less. Jet engines have huge fans inside them that suck in air and compress it. Fuel burns in this air and produces a roaring jet of hot gases that blasts from the rear of the engine, producing thrust. Even more powerful turbojet engines are fitted to some fighter aircraft, but they are noisy and use enormous amounts of fuel.

Passenger jets use turbofan engines that have an extra-large fan at the front of the engine. This fan produces most of the thrust by forcing air around the engine so that it joins up with the jet of exhaust gases at the rear. This surround of cooler air helps to muffle the roar of the jet.

Jet stream
An octopus uses jet propulsion to move along. It sucks in water and squeezes it out through a small hole. The jet of water pushes it along.

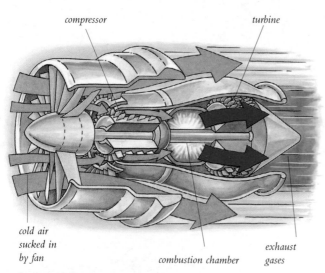

compressor

turbine

cold air sucked in by fan

combustion chamber

exhaust gases

A turbofan engine
Jet engines are naturally tube-shaped because of the shape of the workings inside. Fast-spinning fans compress air into the engine. Fuel burns in the air and heats it. The exhaust gases spin the turbine, a set of blades that drives the compressor. Gases are forced out of the engine at over 2,000m per second and at 1,000°C. The blast of hot gases, together with the surrounding cold air, pushes the engine, and the aircraft, forwards.

Inside a jet engine
A model of an aircraft's jet engine is shown with its protective casing removed so that the internal parts can be seen. The air is drawn into the engine from the left. The blades in the compressor unit then increase the air pressure before the fuel is passed further into the engine and ignited.

Lockheed Blackbird

Executive jet
A small commuter jet can reach speeds of
790km/h – nearly as fast as a large airliner.
It is designed with the engines on the tail,
rather than under the wings. The high
tailplane avoids jet exhausts.

Reconnaissance
The Lockheed SR-71 Blackbird
reconnaissance plane is powered by
turbojet engines. In 1974, one flew from
New York to London in 1 hour, 54 minutes – a
still unbroken record of 3,331km/h. In the 1970s
and 1980s, these aeroplanes were designed to fly fast
and at high altitude specifically for the use of the US Air
Force to take aerial photographs of enemy territory.

Jumbo jet
The Boeing 747
was the first
wide-bodied
jet aeroplane.
It can carry
400 or more
passengers.
Since it was
introduced
in 1970, it
has made
international
jet travel commonplace.

Turboshaft engine
This helicopter is powered by a type
of jet engine without a stream (jet)
of gases. Most of the energy from the
engine turns the rotors providing the
thrust needed to keep it airborne.
Only a tiny bit of energy pushes
the helicopter forwards.

Turboprop engine
The Vickers Viscount was one
of the first and most successful
passenger aircraft powered by jet engines
that turned propellers. It was widely used in
the 1950s and could carry 60 passengers.

ZOOM THROUGH THE AIR

A JET engine produces thrust from a roaring jet of super-hot gas. Its construction looks complicated, but the way it works is very simple. A powerful jet of gas moving in one direction produces thrust in the other direction. Imagine you are standing on a skateboard and squirting a powerful hose forwards. Jet propulsion will push you backwards. This reaction has been known about for nearly 2,000 years, but it was not until the 1930s that it was applied to an engine.

In the first experiment, you can make a jet zoom along a string. The jet engine is a balloon that produces thrust from escaping air. The second project shows you how to make a set of blades called a turbine. It uses hot air to turn the blades. These projects may seem very simple, but they use the same scientific principles that propel all jet aeroplanes through the air. When doing the turbine project ask an adult to light the candles.

Water pressure
As the fruit of the squirting cucumber ripens, the contents become liquid. More water is drawn into it so that the pressure inside increases, like a balloon. Eventually it breaks off the stem and shoots away, squirting the seeds behind it.

BALLOON JET

You will need: long, thin balloon, scissors, sticky tape, drinking straw, string.

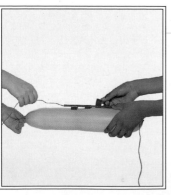

1 Blow up the balloon and, while a friend holds the neck, tape the straw to its top. Thread the string through the straw and, holding it level, tie it to something to keep it in place.

2 Let go of the neck of the balloon. A stream of air jets backwards and produces thrust. This propels the balloon forwards along the string at high speed. Bring the balloon back, blow it up and try another flight.

TURBINE LIGHTS

You will need: *tinfoil pie dish, scissors, pair of compasses, protractor, ruler, dressmaking pin, 8cm length of 3mm diameter dowel, masking tape, bead, cotton reel, non-hardening modelling material, plate, four night lights, matches.*

1 Cut out the bottom of a large tinfoil pie dish as evenly as possible. Make a small hole in the centre with the point of the pair of compasses.

2 Mark a smaller circle in the centre. Mark 16 equal sections as in the spin project and cut along each one to the inner circle. Try to use just one scissor cut along each line.

6 Place the hole in the centre of the turbine over the pin. Ask an adult to light the night lights. Hot air will spin the blades.

3 Angle the blades by holding the inner tip and twisting the outer edges 20 to 30 degrees. The centre of the inner tip should be flat, in line with the centre of the disc.

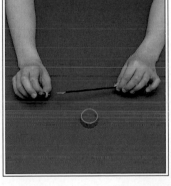

4 Tape the blunt end of the pin to one end of the dowel. Place the bead on the pin. This will allow the turbine to spin freely.

5 Put the dowel in the cotton reel and press the reel into the modelling material in the centre of the plate. Place the four night lights on the plate around the cotton reel.

FASTER THAN SOUND

THE SOUND barrier is like an invisible wall that travels in front of a speeding aircraft. As an aeroplane flies, it sends out pressure waves through the air that are like the ripples streaming from a boat. The waves move away from the aircraft at the speed of sound. When the aircraft is travelling at this speed, the waves cannot outrun it. They build up and compress the air in front of the aircraft.

To fly faster than the speed of sound, the aircraft must fly through this barrier of dense air and overtake it. Wartime pilots, whose planes flew close to the speed of sound in a dive, reported that there seemed to be something slowing them down. The aircraft goes through the sound barrier with a jolt because drag suddenly increases and decreases again. Shock waves spread out and can be heard on the ground as a rumbling sonic boom. This boom represents all the sound energy that otherwise would be spread out in front of the aircraft, all arriving at once. We hear it as a rumble because of the distance it has travelled.

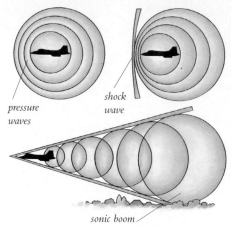

pressure waves

shock wave

sonic boom

Under pressure
As an aircraft flies along, it sends out pressure waves. At the speed of sound, a shock wave builds up in front of the aircraft. As the aircraft accelerates through the sound barrier, the shock wave breaks away to be heard on the ground as a sonic (sound) boom.

Bell X-1

Rocket plane
In 1947, the rocket-powered Bell X-1 was the first aircraft to travel faster than the speed of sound. The thin air at great heights reduces friction, but would not provide a propeller-driven engine with the oxygen in the air that it would need to burn its fuel. A rocket motor was needed for this.

Bombshell
The Bell X-1 rocket plane was dropped from a B29 bomber at 6,000m. This was the highest that a propeller-driven engine could reach. As the pilot accelerated and climbed to a height of 13,000m, the aircraft broke through the sound barrier.

Jet fighter
The Mirage flies at more than twice the speed of sound. It climbs almost straight upwards, speeding faster than a rifle bullet. It can reach the same height as a cruising airliner in about one minute. The Mirage is used by air forces around the world. There are different models for use as fighters, fighter bombers or for reconnaissance.

Pilot's-eye view
A large transparent canopy gives the pilot a good field of view. Fighter pilots need an array of computers in the cockpit to cope with the enormous amounts of information they need to fly their jets safely.

Making waves

The wave created by the front of a boat (pushing through the water) is caused by the same process as the shock wave of a supersonic aircraft. The boat is travelling faster than the natural speed of the wave at the water's surface. The denser the air (or water), the quicker sound can travel through it. So speed of sound is greatest at sea level, where the air is most dense.

FACT BOX
• The speed of sound is described as Mach 1. The actual speed can change, according to air temperature and density. Sound travels faster in warm air. At sea level (20°C), Mach 1 is 1,225km/h, but at 12,000m (−50°C) Mach 1 is 1,060km/h.

• Subsonic speeds are below Mach 0.8 (jumbo jets). Transonic speeds are between Mach 0.8 and Mach 1.2 (breaking the sound barrier). Supersonic speeds are between Mach 1.2 and Mach 5 (Concorde and fighter jets). Hypersonic speeds are above Mach 5 (the space shuttle during re-entry).

• The first supersonic civilian aircraft to fly was the Russian Tupolev Tu-144 on the last day of 1968, two months before Concorde.

Breaking the sound barrier
Concorde is the world's only supersonic passenger aircraft. It cruises at 2,175km/h, over twice the speed of an ordinary airliner, and can cross the Atlantic Ocean in just over three hours. Its engines, however, are noisy and use a lot of fuel.

GOING UP

WATCH A BIRD taking off. It flaps its wings and up it goes! A modern airliner must hurtle down a runway as fast as a racing car. It has to travel up to 3km to reach take-off speed, when its wings lift it off the ground. Some special types of aircraft are designed to take off and land on a single spot. These are called Vertical Take-Off and Landing aircraft (or VTOL for short). Examples include the Harrier jump jet and an early prototype, nicknamed the *Flying Bedstead* because of its very peculiar appearance.

Helicopters are VTOL aircraft, but they are slow compared to aeroplanes and use a lot of fuel. Other aircraft are designed to use very short runways a few hundred metres long. They are called Short Take-Off and Landing aircraft (STOL). They can fly from inner-city airports or from remote airstrips in fields or deserts. Modern aircraft for use on aircraft carriers are now VTOL or STOL fighter planes. For this reason, the flight deck of modern aircraft carriers is much shorter than that of earlier ships. However, these aircraft still use up more fuel than conventional planes.

Up and away
The *Flying Bedstead* from the 1950s was built to experiment with ideas about vertical flight. Moving nozzles directed the thrust from a jet engine. Experiments with this machine helped finalize the design of the Harrier jump jet.

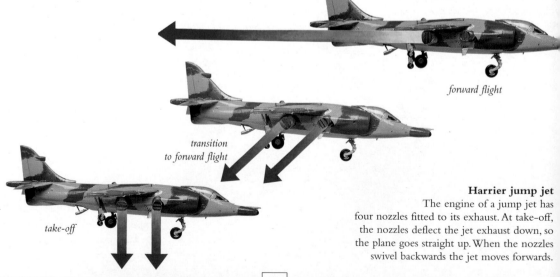

forward flight

transition to forward flight

take-off

Harrier jump jet
The engine of a jump jet has four nozzles fitted to its exhaust. At take-off, the nozzles deflect the jet exhaust down, so the plane goes straight up. When the nozzles swivel backwards the jet moves forwards.

De Havilland Dash
This aircraft is used on short runways in cities. It has four extra-quiet engines and can carry up to 54 passengers. Its large wings provide plenty of lift and are set high on its body to keep the propellers clear off the ground. The Dash can take off on a runway just 700m long.

Autogyro
The autogyro is a cross between an aeroplane and helicopter. The helicopter-type rotor is not driven by the engine. During flight, rushing air spins the rotor which provides most of the lift to keep the autogyro up in the air.

Bell-Boeing Osprey
The Osprey is known as a tilt-rotor aircraft. The giant propellers are called proprotors. These are mounted at the tips of the wings and tilt upwards for take-off, like a helicopter. For forward flight, the proprotors swing into the propeller position of an aeroplane. The Osprey can fly about three times as far as a helicopter on the same fuel load.

Landing on water
Some modern aircraft carriers are much shorter than World War II carriers. They carry short take-off and landing planes such as the Harrier jump jet which need the ski jump ramp at the bow, for almost vertical take off. Some carriers catapult the planes as they take-off from the bow. Such planes land at the stern and are stopped by wires across the deck.

STRANGE AIRCRAFT

MANY AIRCRAFT have strange shapes. The
Belluga looks like an enormous, fat
dolphin with wings. The fabric used to make the
wings of a pedal-powered aircraft is so thin that
light shines through it. In each case, an aircraft's
appearance is due to its being designed for a
particular purpose such as speed or
transportation. The Belluga is designed to carry
large items which will not fit into the cargo hold
of an ordinary transport aeroplane. The wings of
pedal-powered aircraft are covered in thin plastic
films to make them ultralight.

The people who design new planes are called
aeronautical engineers. They can design planes for all sorts of different
purposes – to carry enormous loads, to fly super-fast, or even to fly
non-stop around the world. All aircraft, however, have certain common
requirements – they all must be able to take off, fly straight and level,
and to land safely. Most aircraft are a compromise between many
conflicting factors. They need to carry loads, fly fast and be efficient.
Some aircraft have mostly been designed to be as effective as possible in
just one of these ways at the expense of the others.

On the lookout
The *Optica*
observation plane
was designed for
low-speed flight and
to give a clear view.
It is used to observe
such things as
problems with traffic
flow or crop growth.

Pedal power
Gossamer Albatross was the first pedal-powered
aircraft. It was made of thin plastic stretched on
ribs only 6mm thick to make it light enough
for a strong man to power.

World traveller
In 1986, *Voyager* took nine days to fly Americans Jeana Yeager and
Dick Rutan non-stop around the world without refuelling. Each
wing of the specially built plane was four times the length of the
fuselage, providing the greatest lift with the lowest drag.

Invisible fighter

The F-117 'stealth' fighter is made up of flat, slab-shaped panels and special materials. These scatter beams from enemy radars and make the plane almost undetectable. Ordinary aircraft reflect radar beams straight back so they can be spotted. The F-117's low, flat shape reflects radar waves in directions other than back to the receiver, while special paint absorbs some of the radar waves.

A whale of a plane

The Belluga transport plane can carry almost 25 tonnes of cargo in its 8m-high hold. The Belluga is enormous, but it has the streamlined shape of a dolphin to help reduce drag. The hold is so enormous that it can carry a set of airliner wings from their manufacturers to the assembly point.

Sun strength

Solar Challenger was the world's first solar-powered aircraft. It flew across the English Channel in July 1981, in 5 hours and 23 minutes. Weighing 59kg, it is still the lightest powered aircraft. Solar cells on the wings change sunlight into electricity. An electric motor drives the propellers. A solar powered plane, based on the same ideas, has flown non-stop round the world.

Splash down

In areas near forests like this one in Canada, firefighting planes are used to carry water from the sea or a lake to put out forest fires. Some use an enormous flexible bucket suspended below the plane to pick up the water. Others, like this one, scoop the water directly into the body of the fuselage.

FACT BOX
• In 1907, one of the first British powered flights was made in a bizarre-looking multiplane known as the *Venetian Blind*. It had nearly 50 sets of wings.

• The aircraft with the longest wingspan was a flying boat, the *Spruce Goose*. Designed by eccentric millionaire Howard Hughes, it had a wingspan of over 97m. It made its first and only flight in 1947.

• A flying wing is an aeroplane with no tail or fuselage. The cabin and engines are inside the wing. The Northrop B-2 stealth bomber is an example of a flying wing.

SPEEDING THROUGH WATER

W INGS CAN also work underwater. Some boats have underwater wings called hydrofoils. As the boat speeds along, the aerofoil-shaped hydrofoils lift it out of the water. The hull of the boat is now travelling in the air, so drag is greatly reduced. Hydrofoil boats can travel at 100km/h, over three times as fast as an ordinary boat. Hovercraft seem to fly across the sea, just a few centimetres above the surface. Powerful fans blow air down through a rubber skirt to provide a cushion of air. This cushion cuts down the friction between the hovercraft and the water below. Propellers drive the hovercraft forward at up to 120km/h.

Many birds and even a few insects fly underwater. Penguins are birds that cannot fly in the air but can move so rapidly underwater that they can leap out of the water and even on to ice floes a metre or more above the surface. They don't flap their wings up and down to swim, but use a rowing action. Birds that can fly both above and below the water include auks, such as puffins and guillemots.

Sea skimming
Hydrofoils lift the hull of this craft completely clear of the water. At res it floats on the water like a normal boat. A small hydrofoil lifts a large b because water is more dense than ai and so slower speeds create more lif

HOW A HYDROFOIL WORKS

You will need: *the lid of a margarine tub, scissors, stapler, bradawl, pliers, coat hanger wire (ask an adult to cut out the bottom section).*

1 Cut a rectangle of plastic, about 5cm by 10cm, from the lid of the margarine tub. Fold it in half. Staple the ends together 1cm in from the back edge.

2 Use a bradawl to make two holes in the front of the hydrofoil 1cm away from the folded edge. Use pliers to bend 2cm of one end of the wire. Slide the hydrofoil on to the wire.

3 Make sure that the hydrofoil moves freely on the wire. Try moving your hydrofoil in air – it will not lift up because air is far less dense than water. Pull it through water and it will rise up the wire. Water moves quicker over the hydrofoil than beneath it, reducing the pressure above. The higher pressure below pushes up the hydrofoil.

HOW A HOVERCRAFT WORKS

You will need:
polystyrene tray, pencil, balloon, balloon pump, button.

1 Use a pencil to poke a hole through the middle of the polystyrene tray. The hole should be about 1cm across.

2 Blow up the balloon with the pump. Push its neck through the hole. Keep pinching the neck of the balloon to stop the air escaping.

4 Place the tray on a table. Air escapes steadily from under the tray's edges, lifting it up a few millimetres. Give the tray a gentle push and it will skate along.

3 Keep pinching with one hand, using the other hand to slip the button into the neck. The button will control how fast the air escapes.

Water spray
A hovercraft's rubber skirt is the black part just above the water. You can see how the air cushion makes the water spray about. Four large propellers drive the hovercraft in any direction. Hovercraft work best if the water is not too rough. They are used for travel along rivers and lakes, but some are still used on the sea.

FLYING THROUGH SPACE

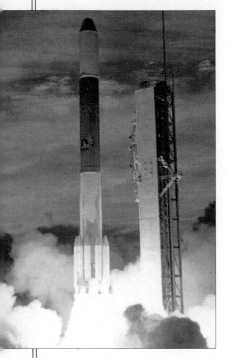

SPACE ROCKETS rely on jet propulsion to fly. A stream of hot gases roars out from the tail end and the rocket surges forward. Deep under the sea, octopuses rely on jet propulsion to escape from their enemies. They squirt out a jet of water and shoot off in the opposite direction. This project shows you how to make and fly a rocket that uses jet propulsion. The thrust of a rocket depends on the mass of propellant it shoots out every second. Water is a much better propellant than hot gas because it is so much heavier. Follow these instructions carefully and your rocket could fly to over 25m above the ground. You may need adult help to make some parts of this rocket and to launch it. When you are ready for a test flight, set your rocket up in an open space, well away from trees and buildings. This rocket is very powerful – you must not stand over it while it is being launched. Wear clothes that you do not mind getting very wet!

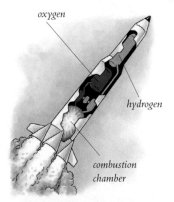

oxygen

hydrogen

combustion chamber

Inside the rocket
Liquid hydrogen and liquid oxygen are pumped into the combustion chamber. The hydrogen burns furiously in the oxygen. The exhaust produces immense thrust.

Satellite launch
Rockets with powerful engines can carry satellites into orbit 320km or more above the Earth's surface.

MAKE A ROCKET

You will need: card, pen, coloured card, scissors, plastic bottle, strong sticky tape, funnel, jug of water, cork, bradawl, air valve, plastic tubing, bicycle pump.

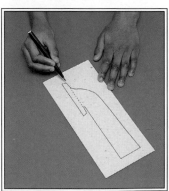

1 Rockets have fins to make them fly straight. Draw out this fin template (it is about 20 cm long) on to plain card and use it to cut out four fins from coloured card.

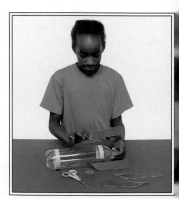

2 Decorate your bottle to look like a rocket. Fold over the tab at the top of each fin. Use long pieces of strong sticky tape to firmly attach the fins to the bottle.

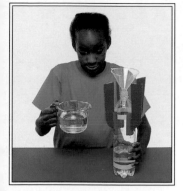

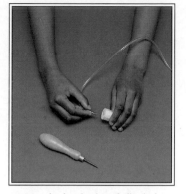

3 Use the funnel to half-fill the bottle with water. (The water is the propellant. Compressed air above the water will provide the energy that makes the thrust.)

4 Use the bradawl to drill a hole through the cork. Push the wide end of the air valve into the plastic tubing. Push the valve through the hole in the cork.

5 Hold the bottle with one hand and push the cork and the valve into the neck of the bottle using the other hand. Push it in firmly so the cork does not slide out too easily.

7 Stand the rocket on its tail fins. Start pumping. Bubbles of air will rise up through the water. When the pressure in the bottle gets high enough, the cork and water will be forced out and the rocket will fly upwards.

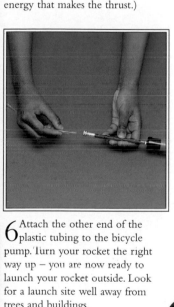

6 Attach the other end of the plastic tubing to the bicycle pump. Turn your rocket the right way up – you are now ready to launch your rocket outside. Look for a launch site well away from trees and buildings.

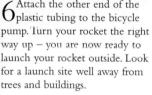

BIRDS IN FLIGHT

MUSCLE-POWERED flight is very hard work. In the past, many people have tried to fly by flapping artificial wings but no-one has succeeded. Birds, however, are very light and powerful compared to us, and are perfectly designed to stay up in the air. Birds' wings are covered in feathers – one of the strongest and lightest natural materials known. The aerofoil shape of their wings provides lift, while tail feathers help with steering and braking. Birds flap their wings hard to take off and climb into the air, and need enormous flight muscles to provide enough power for flight. These muscles account for nearly a quarter of the weight of some birds, for example eagles. To make sure plenty of blood is pumped to the muscles as they work, birds also have a large, fast-beating heart. If humans were to fly, they would need a chest the size of a barrel, arms 3m long, legs like broom handles, and a head the size of an apple – as well as thousands of feathers!

barb

Light as a feather
Every feather has a hollow tube running down its centre. Microscopic hooks lock each barb together so that air cannot pass through.

Eagle in flight
A soaring bird such as a vulture or an eagle has spread-out feathers with slots in between. Each feather acts as a tiny aerofoil, lifting the bird as it flies through the air.

primary feathers

Flying feathers
The large primary flight feathers on the end of each wing produce most of the power for flight. These feathers can be closed together or spread apart to control flight. Smaller feathers on the inner wing form the curve that provides lift and are known as secondary flight feathers. The innermost feathers keep the bird warm and shape the wing into the bird's body, helping to prevent turbulence in flight.

secondary feathers

On the wing

This sequence of pictures shows how an owl flies through the air. A bird's wings bend in the middle as they rise upwards and the feathers open to let air pass through the wings. On the powerful downstroke, the primary flight feathers slice through the air and the feathers close up again. This pushes the air down and back and pulls the bird upwards and forwards.

flight feathers

wing
bone

flight
muscles

breastbone

A bird's body

Flight feathers are connected to thin bones at the end of each wing. Bird bones are light – most are hollow and filled with air. The large flight muscles are anchored to the breastbone at the front of a bird's chest.

Deadly speed

Peregrine falcons are the fastest animals in the world. They fold back their wings to reduce drag, then dive at their prey at speeds up to 350km/h. The force of the impact breaks the victim's neck instantly.

HOW BIRDS FLY

L OOK AT a large bird, such as a goose, in the sky. Can you describe how its wings are moving? Flying birds do not simply flap their wings up and down. Their wings are not stiff and flat – instead, each wing has a joint like an elbow in the middle. This joint allows the wing to twist upwards on the downstroke and downwards on the upstroke. The feathers on the part of the wing corresponding to your hand are called the primary or flight feathers. On the downstroke, the front edge of the hand is tilted downwards, so that the effect of the air flow is to generate a forward thrust as well as to produce lift. On the upstroke, the front edge is tilted upwards. One effect of this is to produce a downwards force (called anti–lift), but it also produces forward thrust. Thrust propels the bird forward.

Move your hand across and back in a tank of water, with the palm flat. Now tilt your thumb side downwards as you move it across. You can feel the forces pushing against your hand.

As you bring your hand back, tilt the thumb side upwards. The forces are now pushing in different directions. In each case, a force pushes the thumb-edge forward.

A BIRD OF YOUR OWN

You will need: *sheets of stiff paper, sticky tape, scissors, glue stick.*

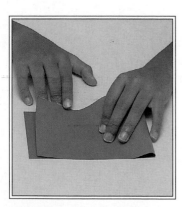

1 Start by making the bird's short legs. Fold one piece of paper in half lengthways. Fold it again several times until the paper is about 2.5cm across.

2 Fold the strip of paper in half, as shown, and make a fold at each end for the feet. Tape the feet to your work surface to help keep your model stable.

3 To make the body of your bird, roll a piece of paper into a tube and secure the edge with adhesive tape. Use some more tape to stick the body to the legs.

4 To make the wings, fold a piece of paper twice lengthways so that it is about six times longer than it is wide. Fold it into a W shape.

5 Stick the wings on to the body. You have now made a model bird. To mimic how a bird flies, hold one wing tip in each hand.

6 Move your hands in circles – one going clockwise, the other anticlockwise. At take-off, a bird's wings make large, round circles.

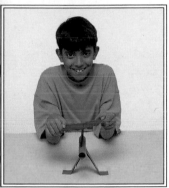

7 During the upstroke, notice how the bird's wings bend in the middle. Some birds raise their wings so high at the top of the upstroke that they bang together.

8 During the downstroke, the wings become flatter. To see how a bird's wings move when the bird is flying level, place your hands farther apart and move the wings in small, flat circles.

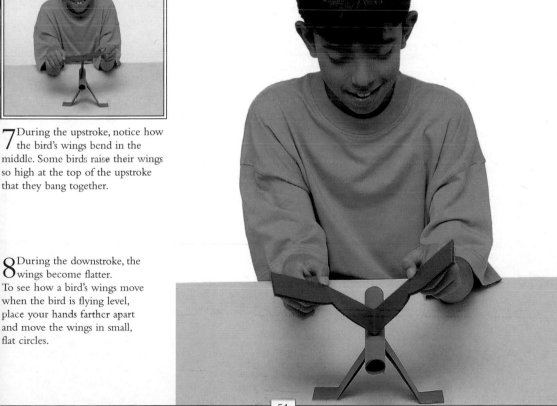

INSECT WINGS

Hollow wings
As with all insects, a dragonfly's wings are thin and light. They are strengthened by a network of hollow tubes, called veins.

Dragonfly darter

INSECTS ARE generally smaller than birds, though some large hawk moths are bigger than some hummingbirds. Insects' wings are flat and stiff, and do not curve into the aerofoil shape. The smaller an insect is, the more important the effects of air resistance become. This drag slows an insect down, but also stops it from sinking downwards.

Although the flight of large insects such as dragonflies may appear to be similar to that of birds, it is not. Insects use their wings to propel themselves through the air. Most flying insects, such as bees, dragonflies and moths, have two pairs of wings. Some, such as true flies and mosquitos, only have one pair and are the most agile fliers. Others, such as hover-flies, can hover and then dart off in any direction, twisting and turning through the air. Their second wings act as a weight that manoeuvres them in different directions. They can even fly backwards.

1 The dragonfly is one of the most skilled flying insects. Most insects flap their wings in the same motion, but a dragonfly uses its two pairs of wings separately.

2 The dragonfly beats its front wings down to stir up a whirlwind. This passes over the back wings, generating lift. The dragonfly uses its long, flexible body to steer.

3 With each beat, the wings push air down and back, moving the dragonfly up and forward. The wings bend as they flap, to give more control in flight.

Butterflies

The two pairs of wings on butterflies are hooked together so they act like one. Many butterflies have square-shaped wings that flap quite slowly. Their wings are covered with powdery coloured scales. The largest butterflies have wingspans up to 28cm across.

Beetle wings

The front wings of a beetle are hard covers that protect the flying wings underneath. In flight, the wing covers stick out, helping to steady the beetle's body.

Haltères

Instead of a second pair of wings, crane flies have tiny club-like structures called haltères. These act as stabilizers, and allow them to perform their astonishing aerobatics.

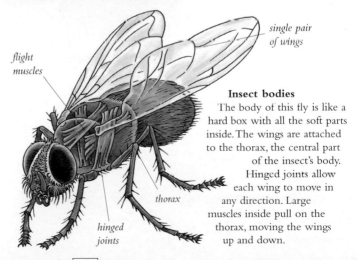

flight muscles

single pair of wings

Insect bodies

The body of this fly is like a hard box with all the soft parts inside. The wings are attached to the thorax, the central part of the insect's body. Hinged joints allow each wing to move in any direction. Large muscles inside pull on the thorax, moving the wings up and down.

thorax

hinged joints

AMAZING FLYING ANIMALS

Bats are the only animals that can fly, apart from birds and insects. They have wings that can push downwards to create lift. Unlike birds, most bats are nocturnal – they fly at night and sleep in the day. Some other animals can glide through the air, but cannot control or power their flight with flapping wings. Instead, animals such as flying frogs, honey gliders, lizards, snakes and squirrels glide down. They jump outwards from high places like trees and cave walls, moving forwards through the air as they parachute downwards. These animals usually have loose flaps of skin attached to their bodies. The flaps of skin act like the envelope of a parachute, catching the air and enabling controlled descent. Flying fish escape from their enemies and predators just below the ocean surface by sailing through the air above. Their gliding flight only lasts a few seconds, but it is faster than the fish's swimming speed.

Wings and fins
Flying fish swim very fast, close to the surface of the water. With wing-shaped fins stretched out, they leap upwards and forwards into the air, thrashing the water with their tails until they reach take-off.

Parachute tactics
Flying frogs have enormous webbed feet. They use their feet as parachutes when they jump down from trees in search of insects. They alter the shape of their feet to control their flight. There are sticky pads on their toes to help them climb. Using these pads, they can cling to the smoothest leaves and branches in the rainforest.

FACT BOX
• Some flying fish can glide along at 50km/h for several hundred metres. The longest recorded flight for a flying fish lasted 90 seconds and covered more than 1km.

• Flying foxes are actually a type of large fruit-eating bat. There are more than 2,000 species, or types, of bat living in the world.

• Flying snakes are able to flatten their bodies to help them glide from tree to tree.

• Some flying frogs jump from a height of 40m. They glide along, covering about 30m in only 8 seconds.

• The colugo, or flying lemur, can easily glide for at least 100m between trees.

Life-saving spines

A flying lizard has flaps of skin along each side of its body. These are supported by spines hinged to the ribs. When danger threatens, the spines stick out and the lizard glides away.

Tree gliding

Flying squirrels have folds of thin skin between their front and rear legs. They glide from tree to tree by stretching out their legs to spread the skin wide.

Smooth as honey

Honey gliders (*Petaurus breviceps*), are small mammals that sail through the rainforests of Queensland and New Guinea. They eat sweet sap (sucked from trees) and nectar (from flowers).

Flexibility

A bat's wing is a sheet of flexible skin stretched between its fingers, the side of its body and the back of its legs. Bats can alter the shape of their wings much more than birds. They can twist and turn like acrobats in the air as they chase insects for food. The largest bats have wingspans up to 2m, but weigh only 1kg.

PREHISTORIC FLYERS

THE EARLIEST known flying creature is the dragonfly. The first ones lived about 350 million years ago, during a hot, swampy time called the Carboniferous Period. Many other flying insects evolved during the next 150 million years, many of them similar to the insects we know today. The first gliding reptiles appeared about 50 million years later than the first dragonflies. Several different gliding species evolved, such as *Longisquama*. Some of them evolved true flight and became the winged reptiles called pterosaurs. The largest pterosaurs had wingspans up to 12m across.

Over 150 million years ago, the first feathered creature, Archaeopteryx, lived on Earth. Scientists think it evolved from small dinosaurs and may be the first known bird.

Fossilized
This insect lived about 50 million years ago. It was caught in sticky tree resin. The resin gradually fossilized and changed into amber.

FACT BOX

• Some prehistoric dragonflies had wingspans of up to a metre across.

• The earliest humans lived less than one million years ago. Modern-looking birds have existed for over 30 million years.

• Modern birds have just two finger bones in each wing. *Archaeopteryx* had all five, complete with claws at the ends.

• Fish fossils are often found near pterosaurs, so these flying lizards may have lived at sea.

• The largest flying animal ever to have existed was a pterosaur called *Quetzalocoatlus*. It had a human-sized body and a wingspan of 12m – wider than a hang-glider.

Gliding reptiles
The first flying reptiles were gliders. At first there were many different ways of gliding. *Longisquama* had tall crests along its back that might have opened up like wings to help it glide. Scientists now think that the crests were actually ribs. When it rested, it probably held them above its back, like a butterfly. This could also have helped the cold-blooded reptile warm up in the sun so that it could chase insects to eat.

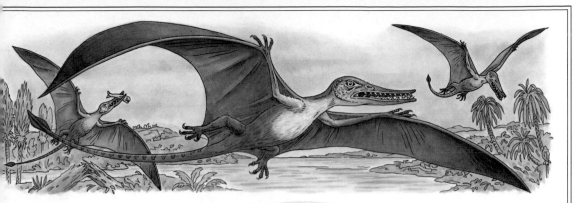

Flying reptiles

The first true flying reptiles were the pterosaurs. They lived at the same time as the dinosaurs and could reach huge sizes. Their wings were made of skin and their bodies were usually furry. The pterosaurs had light, delicate bones that reduced their weight and helped them fly.

Giant pterosaurs

Quetzalocoatlus was a huge pterosaur. It probably flew over dry land and fed, like modern vultures, on carrion. Like the vultures of today, it would have had difficulty taking off from the ground with a full stomach.

Archaeopteryx

Archaeopteryx had bird-like wings and legs, but a mouth full of teeth and a tail like a lizard. It was thickly feathered, but many scientists think it could not fly very well. The first fossilized *Archaeopteryx* was found in a quarry in Germany in 1860. Since then six more have been discovered.

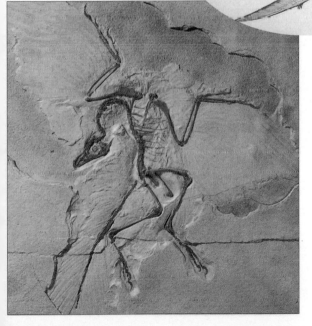

Fossilized feathers

This is a fossilized skeleton of an *Archaeopteryx*. When the animal died, all the skin and flesh rotted away. By studying fossils scientists can learn how ancient animals moved and flew.

THE HISTORY OF FLIGHT

SINCE ANCIENT times, human beings have wanted to fly. The first people to get off the ground were the Chinese who used kites to lift people into the air over 700 years ago. In the 1760s, lighter-than-air balloons carried their first passengers and in 1852, the world's first airship flight occurred. But it was not until the invention of the petrol engine in the 1880s that true powered flight in a heavier-than-air machine became possible. In 1903, the Wright brothers made the world's first powered, controlled and sustained flight in their aircraft, *Flyer 1*. The basic structure of an aeroplane as devised by the Wright brothers has continued to the present day, although many details have changed. The designs of today are thanks to a mix of modern strong and lightweight metals (alloys) used to make planes, and improvements in fuel and engines.

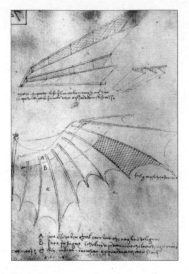

Ahead of time
More than 500 years ago, the Italian artist and inventor Leonardo da Vinci drew designs for flying machines. His ideas about flight were basically correct. However, a human would not have been able to provide enough power to make his machines work.

Clément Ader
In 1890, Ader's steam-driven aircraft *Eole* became the first full-sized aeroplane to leave the ground. It managed to hop 50m. However, it was not considered true powered flight because it was uncontrolled. Before the Wright brothers' success, aircraft wings were modelled on those of birds and bats. These wings are able to twist and move because they are made of separate bones. Such a mechanism does not work when scaled up to a size big enough to carry a man.

Otto Lilienthal
In the 1890s, German experimenter Otto Lilienthal built hang gliders from reeds covered with shirt material. He made over 2,000 flights and showed how curved aerofoil wings work better than flat ones. He was the first person to make repeated, controlled flights, but while making a test flight, Lilienthal crash-landed and died.

Orville and Wilbur Wright

On 17 December 1903, American inventor Orville Wright flew *Flyer 1* for 36m at a height of about 3m. This was the first controlled, powered take-off, flight and landing. The Wright brothers continued to improve their aircraft and eventually their planes could fly for around an hour. Within six years, they were being used by pilots in France and the United States.

Louis Blériot

The Frenchman Louis Blériot designed and built a series of planes. In 1909, he became the first person to fly across the English Channel. At an average speed of 60km/h the journey took 37 minutes. He reported that he had to wrestle constantly with the controls to keep his monoplane flying steadily. Shortly after his flight, a new engine allowed faster speeds and greater stability. The picture shows a modern replica of his plane.

FACT BOX
- 1908 Orville Wright made the first sustained, powered flight lasting one hour.

- 1937 the jet engine was designed by British engineer Frank Whittle.

- 1939 American engineer Igor Sikorsky designed the first helicopter.

- 1947 the first aircraft flew at supersonic speed in the USA.

- 1952 the first jet airliner, the De Havilland Comet, entered service in the UK.

- 1970 Boeing 747 jumbo jet entered service.

- 1976 Concorde started transatlantic service.

Charles Lindbergh

In 1927, American Charles Lindbergh was the first person to fly alone and non-stop across the Atlantic Ocean in his tiny Ryan monoplane, *The Spirit of St Louis*. He took 33 hours and 39 minutes to fly 5,800km from New York to Paris, at an average speed of 173km/h. Lindbergh's feat paved the way for transtlantic passenger services. He became an advisor to the US Air Force and to commercial airlines.

FLY INTO THE FUTURE

Bᴵᴿᴰˢ ʜᴀᵛᴇ been flying for more than 30 million years. Humans took to the air in kites 700 years ago, in balloons only in the 1760s, and in aeroplanes 100 years ago. Now the air is full of aircraft of all descriptions. You can fly half-way around the world in less than 24 hours. Some planes fly three times faster than sound. When you look up into the sky in ten years' time, what will you see? Engineers are developing new and more powerful engines, new materials that are lighter and stronger than metal, and strange new wing shapes to help aircraft fly ever faster and higher. Whatever happens, human flight will continue to develop, probably at heavy cost to the health of our environment and the birds and animals who share it. However, efforts are now being made to reduce the damage.

Jumbo jet
This Boeing 747–400 can carry up to 567 passengers. It is the double-decker version of the 1970s jumbo jet. Plans for a super jumbo, the 747-600X, include an on-board fitness centre and a cinema.

Up, up and away
The Roton is still under development. It claims to be an entirely new approach to space flight. It will use a turbo-driven propeller to rise into the upper atmosphere. It then becomes rocket-powered. On landing the process is reversed.

Horizontal take-off
An artist's impression shows HOTOL, an aircraft that takes off and lands horizontally, riding piggy-back to a height of 15,000m on the *Antonin 225*, the world's largest aeroplane. The HOTOL then launches into Space using rocket engines. Travelling at Mach 5, it could fly from the UK to Australia in under four hours.

FACT BOX
• A Russian experimental plane, called the Aquatain, has been designed to gain extra lift by skimming across the surface of the ocean. The craft is reported to use much less fuel than a conventional aircraft.

• All new aeroplanes have to meet strict environmental rules governing noise levels and emissions that might further damage the sensitive ozone layer.

• Modern cockpits use advanced systems to reduce the pilot's workload. Holographic displays and keyboards project data on to a see-through screen. Optical fibres carry signals at the speed of light to the aircraft's control surfaces.

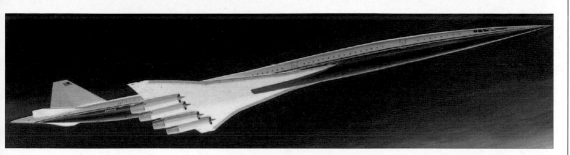

High speed civil transport

Although modern aeroplanes are very efficient, they still contribute enormously to the pollution of the upper atmosphere. Flying at Mach 3, this airliner may one day carry 200 passengers from New York to Tokyo in about three hours. Cruising above 18,000m, it will have low pollutant engines that will not damage the ozone layer.

Space plane

Aircraft can travel extremely fast in Space because there is no air to create drag. This model shows what the X-30 Space plane might look like, flying at speeds up to Mach 5 through the edge of Space to reach its destination. The plane does not have to reach escape velocity (11km/second) as spacecraft do. It can fly to the edge of the atmosphere reaching Mach 5, then cruise through space in an arch, descending again at the end of the journey. At such high speed, extremely thin air on the borders of space provides enough lift to keep it up.

Experimental plane

The X-29 aircraft refuels in mid-air from a large tanker plane. The X-29 has unusual swept-forward wings. These give high lift and low drag making the plane very manoeuvrable. Tests with the X-29 may lead to new designs for passenger planes. The swept-forward wings bear a strange resemblance to *Sharovipteryx*, one of the earliest gliding reptiles. This species differed from other gliders in that the wing was supported by the hind limbs. Scientists studying this fossil think that it also had extended flaps at the front, as in the X-29.

GLOSSARY

aerofoil
Solid object such as a wing, shaped so that there is a pressure difference on the two sides when moving through air.

aeroplane
A heavier-than-air flying machine that includes its own power source.

aileron
A moveable flap on the trailing (rear) edge of an aircraft wing (or other aerofoil) that changes the flow of air across the surfaces.

airbrake
Anything that will rapidly slow an aircraft down using air resistance. It can be either a flap at the rear edge of a wing that can bend down, or a parachute set out behind an aircraft.

alloy
A mixture of metals. Aircraft alloys combine the strength of one metal (such as titanium) with the lightness of another (such as aluminium or magnesium).

angle of attack
The angle between the lower surface of an aerofoil and the direction in which it is moving.

autopilot
A computerized or mechanical system that senses changes in an aircraft's course and automatically adjusts the controls to maintain the original course.

bank
To incline an aircraft at an angle, as part of a turn. An aircraft turning left would bank so that the right wingtip was higher than the left one.

barbs
The projections from the main axis of a feather that comprise the flat surface. Each barb bears interlocking projections binding it to one each side.

biplane
An aircraft with two sets of wings, one above the other.

boomerang
A throwing stick that will return to the thrower if it does not hit anything.

cockpit
The region around the pilot's seat in an aircraft (usually at the front of the aircraft) containing the controls and the instruments.

cruise
To fly at the most efficient speed and height for the design of the aircraft. The cruising speed and height is the one that uses least fuel for the distance covered.

drag
Any force that acts in the opposite direction to motion. Most mechanisms that generate lift also generate drag.

elevator
A moveable flap on the tailplane or rear wing of an aircraft that will cause the nose to rise or fall.

fly
To move through the air in a controlled manner. True flight involves some form of thrust to counter the drag so as to keep moving and maintain or increase height.

fuselage
The main body of an aircraft to which the wings and tail are attached.

glide
A form of flight which is controlled, but which does not have any source of power to counter drag.

halteres
Little stalks, with knobs on the end, found on flies in place of a pair of rear wings. Used to help stabilize their flight.

hang-glider
A very basic form of gliding aircraft. It consists of a wing with a framework for the pilot hanging below.

helium
The second lightest of all gases. It is used for filling lighter-than-air balloons.

hydrofoil
Any solid object that will cause a pressure difference on the two sides when moving through water.

jumbo jet
A passenger aircraft that can carry several hundred people. They are often wide-bodied, with ten or more seats across.

kite
A tethered aerofoil that uses the wind blowing across it to generate lift.

launch
To thrust an aircraft into the air using forces outside the aircraft itself.

lift
The force generated by an aerofoil that counters the force of gravity and keeps the flying object in the air.

monoplane
An aircraft with a single pair of wings, one either side.

ozone layer
The layer of the upper atmosphere, about 20km above the Earth's surface, where ozone is formed. It filters ultraviolet rays from the Sun.

parachute
To descend from a height with control over the speed of descent, with limited control over direction.

paraglider
A glider with a wing inflated by air entering its leading edge. The pilot steers from side to side and rides up thermals.

pitch
Either: A change in the vertical direction of flight either up or down; or: the angle at which a propellor blade is set.

port
The left-hand side of a boat or aircraft when facing forward.

reconnaissance
Surveying and searching over an unknown area, especially to guide following travellers.

resistance
A force that counters another. Air resistance (or drag) is caused by frictional forces of the air passing over an aircraft's surface countering engine thrust.

roll
A sideways tilting movement of an aircraft.

rotor
A set of inclined blades radiating from a central block that can rotate.

rudder
A flap set in the vertical part of the tail fin, which can control the direction of the aircraft.

slat
A flat piece at the front of the wing which can move out to increase the surface area.

soar
To maintain height whilst gliding by using air currents such as thermals.

spoiler
An airbrake formed from a hinged flap on the rear edge of a wing.

starboard
The right-hand side of a boat or aircraft when facing forward.

streamlined
A shape that moves through air (or water) in the most efficient manner, with the least frictional resistance.

supersonic
An airspeed faster than that of sound.

tailplane
The small horizontal wings at the rear of an aircraft.

tether
A cord that attaches a flying object to the ground, as in a kite.

thermal
A rising current of air formed when a part of the ground surface is heated by the sun. This warms up the air just above the ground, which then rises.

thorax
The part of the body between the head and abdomen. In insects, the thorax bears the legs and wings.

throwing stick
A bent and aerofoil-shaped stick that can be thrown far and accurately.

thrust
The force that pushes an aircraft or flying animal forwards.

triplane
An aircraft with three sets of wings, one above the other.

turbine
A rotor that is moved by fast-moving gas currents. In aircraft, this air current is generated by burning fuel to produce hot, fast-moving gas.

turbofan
A jet engine in which much of the turbine rotation is used to drive a fan that pushes air round the central engine. The thrust comes from the turbine jet exhaust and the fan-driven air.

turbojet
A form of jet engine in which the turbine jet provides all the thrust.

turboprop
A form of jet engine in which most of the rotation of the turbine is used to drive a propeller which then propels the aircraft.

turboshaft
A form of jet engine in which all of the rotation of the turbine is used to drive a rotor which then propels the aircraft. Used particularly in helicopters.

turbulence
Air movement that consists of eddies in random directions, with no smooth flow of air.

undercarriage
The landing wheels of an aircraft. In some aircraft the undercarriage can be lifted during flight to reduce drag.

upthrust
An upwards force on an object in air or water that generates lift.

windsock
A tubular kite on a short tether that is used to indicate wind direction and strength.

yaw
A change in the horizontal direction of flight, either left or right.

Index